HERO JOURNALS

Alexander the Great

Nick Hunter

Raintree is an imprint of Capstone Global Library Limited, a company incorporated in England and Wales having its registered office at 7 Pilgrim Street, London, EC4V 6LB – Registered company number: 6695582

www.raintreepublishers.co.uk
myorders@raintreepublishers.co.uk

Text © Capstone Global Library Limited 2014
First published in hardback in 2014
Paperback edition first published in 2015
The moral rights of the proprietor have been asserted.

Edited by Adam Miller, Charlotte Guillain, and Claire Throp
Designed by Richard Parker
Original illustrations © Capstone Global Library Ltd 2014
Illustrated by Florence Faure (Advocate Art)
Picture research Tracy Cummins
Production by Victoria Fitzgerald
Originated by Capstone Global Library Ltd
Printed and bound in China by CTPS

ISBN 978 1 406 26568 2 (hardback)
17 16 15 14 13
10 9 8 7 6 5 4 3 2 1

ISBN 978 1 406 26575 0 (paperback)
18 17 16 15 14
10 9 8 7 6 5 4 3 2 1

British Library Cataloguing in Publication Data
Hunter, Nick
Alexander the Great. – (Hero journals)
938'.07'092-dc23
A full catalogue record for this book is available from the British Library.

Acknowledgements
We would like to thank the following for permission to reproduce photographs: Art Resource, NY pp. 4 (© Gilles Mermet), 7 (© Gianni Dagli Orti), 23 (© Alfredo Dagli Orti/ The Art Archive), 26 (© RMN-Grand Palais), 33 (The Art Archive); Bridgeman Art Library pp. 14 (© Look and Learn), 25 (De Agostini Picture Library/A. Dagli Orti), 32 (National Geographic Image Collection), 36 (© The Stapleton Collection), 37 (© Padovanino, Alessandro (1588–1648)/Hermitage, St Petersburg, Russia); Corbis pp. 15 (© Araldo de Luca), 19 (© Bettmann); Getty Images pp. 21 (DeAgostini), 24 (SSPL), 30 (Travel Ink), 39 (Leemage); Shutterstock pp. 11 (Panos Karapanagiotis), 12 (Federico Rostagno), 16 (Panos Karapanagiotis), 17 (Paul Picone), 28 (arazu). Design features reproduced with permission of Shutterstock (R-studio, Pavel K, Picsfive, karawan).

Cover photograph of a statue of Alexander the Great as the Greek god Helios reproduced with permission of Art Resource, NY (bpk, Berlin/Art Resource).

Every effort has been made to contact copyright holders of material reproduced in this book. Any omissions will be rectified in subsequent printings if notice is given to the publisher.

All the internet addresses (URLs) given in this book were valid at the time of going to press. However, due to the dynamic nature of the internet, some addresses may have changed, or sites may have changed or ceased to exist since publication. While the author and publisher regret any inconvenience this may cause readers, no responsibility for any such changes can be accepted by either the author or the publisher.

Contents

Who is Alexander the Great?

When you see "the Great" after someone's name, you know they were probably pretty special. To build an empire stretching from Europe to India, you have to be a truly great leader. If you can do it by the time you're 32 years old, then people are going to remember you for thousands of years. My name is Alexander, and I am that man.

Don't get me wrong; I had a good start in life. It's a lot easier building an empire when you start off as the son of a king. But that didn't mean I had everything handed to me on a plate. When my father died, his enemies thought I'd be a pushover. They soon found out the truth.

They put up statues of me across Europe, North Africa, and Asia.

4

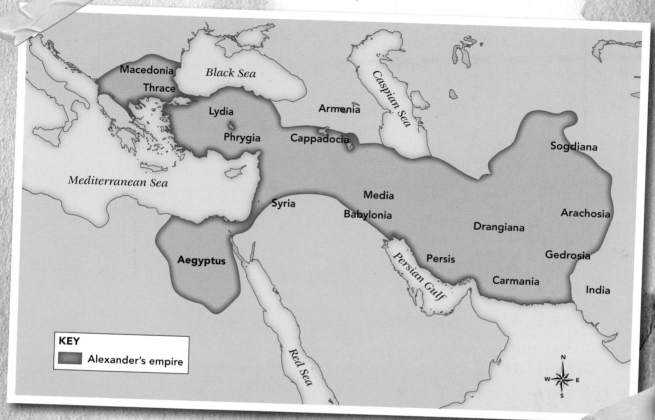

Macedonia
Thrace
Black Sea
Lydia
Armenia
Caspian Sea
Phrygia
Cappadocia
Sogdiana
Mediterranean Sea
Media
Syria
Babylonia
Drangiana
Arachosia
Aegyptus
Persis
Gedrosia
Persian Gulf
Carmania
India

KEY
Alexander's empire

Red Sea

N
W E
S

What's next?

Building empires is all very well but I was really an explorer and a man of action. I was never satisfied with just ruling my home country of Macedonia, or even Greece or Egypt. I was always thinking about the next land or enemy to conquer. I suppose you could say I didn't know when to stop.

Document it!

Alexander the Great achieved incredible things at a very young age. His victories have been celebrated throughout history. If you keep a journal, you can record your own successes and ambitions, including what you think and feel about them.

A boy with a big future

From the day I was born around 20 July 356 BC, people started making up stories about me. Some said that I was the son of Zeus, the chief of the Greek gods. Others said that my mother had dreamed of being struck by a thunderbolt before I was born.

It's always nice to be talked about, but I think most of these stories were invented by my mother, Olympias. She was a Greek princess who could be very tough and cunning. I spent my childhood in Pella, Macedonia with Mum and my sister Cleopatra.

What about Dad? Well Dad, or King Philip II of Macedonia as most people called him, was never around much. Even the day I was born he was off fighting a battle.

Mighty Macedonia?

Macedonia claimed to be one of the Greek city-states, like Athens and Sparta to the south, but many Greeks were not so sure. They thought the warlike Macedonians were barbarians. However, when Alexander was young, his father was in the process of uniting the Macedonians into a powerful military force.

Philip II of Macedonia

Alexander's father was a formidable soldier in his own right. He established Macedonia as the most powerful country in the region, and was chosen to lead Greek forces against their biggest enemy – the Persian Empire.

Education

King Philip may have preferred spending time with his armies than his family, but he wanted to make sure I had a good education. Macedonians were great fighters, but if you wanted teachers, Athens was the best place to find them. Greek teachers, artists, and scientists often visited Pella, and I listened to everything they could tell me.

Lessons were all very well, but I really wanted to see some action. My father was always fighting one war or another and I couldn't wait until it was my time. I loved wrestling, riding, and hunting with my friends.

Bucephalus

When I was 12 years old, I finally managed to impress my father. He had been given a horse that no one could tame. This was my chance to prove myself to the old warrior. I trained Bucephalus well, and he went on to be my warhorse for most of my life.

The Greek world

Ancient Greece was not one country. It was made up of several city-states, of which the most powerful were Athens, Sparta, and Thebes. By the time of Alexander's birth, the states' power was declining. They would soon be under the control of Macedonia. However, Greece's art and ideas still had a powerful influence on the ancient world.

This map shows Macedonia and the Greek states around the time of my birth.

Top teacher

The best teacher I ever had was Aristotle. You wouldn't have expected us to get on. Aristotle liked to think and study the world around him, while I was more likely to act first and think later. But he really opened my eyes on subjects from politics to science. Later, I would always try to send plants and other things from my travels back to my old teacher.

Storytelling

I loved the amazing Greek stories I learned with Aristotle. My favourites were the stories of Homer. The *Iliad* told the story of a war between Greece and Troy. Another great story was the *Odyssey*, in which Odysseus comes home from Troy by the scenic route. Soon I'd be setting off on a long journey of my own.

Aristotle didn't just teach me. He also taught my friends, Nearchus and Hephaestion, who stayed with me long after I'd stopped playing and had begun my real battles.

"[The young] are passionate and quick tempered, they follow their impulses, they are ruled by their emotions. They strive for honour, especially for victory, and desire them both much more than money."

Aristotle's thoughts about young people. Was he thinking of his pupil Alexander?

Aristotle

Aristotle was not just Alexander's teacher, he was also one of the greatest thinkers in history. He spent much of his childhood at the royal court in Macedonia before joining the Academy of the great thinker Plato in Athens. Aristotle's ideas shaped the study of science just as much as Alexander's conquests shaped the world.

The teenage regent

By the time I was 16, I really thought I knew it all. I'd had the best teachers that Macedonian gold could buy. I could fight and hunt as well as anyone; now I just needed a job. My father was always planning the next war, so he left me in charge of Macedonia.

I decided to begin by taking an army to give the nearby Thracians a good thrashing. I even set up a new city there. It's always tough coming up with names, but I thought Alexandroúpolis had a good ring to it.

My father was turning his attention to Greece. They may have been clever, but they were no match for the mighty Macedonian army. We defeated a Greek army at the Battle of Chaeronea. I got to visit Athens. It was an impressive city, but the Athenians now had to do what the Macedonians told them.

Macedonians were too busy fighting to worry about creating great buildings like the Parthenon in Athens.

Olympias

Alexander's mother was a strong woman in her own right, and she did not always see eye to eye with King Philip. When the Macedonian king chose to marry a younger woman as well as her, Olympias took Alexander to live with her brother. After Philip's death, Olympias returned to Macedonia and ordered her rival wife to be murdered.

The League of Corinth

By 338 BC, Philip had made it clear that he was now in charge of all the Greek city-states. He made this formal when he organized them into a group called the League of Corinth, with Philip in charge. The first thing they decided was that Philip would lead a combined Greek and Macedonian army against the Persian Empire.

Disputes with Dad

No sooner had he sorted out the Greeks than my father was planning his next campaign. Seriously, this man did not know when to quit! He was planning an expedition against the giant Persian Empire.

The worst thing was, he wasn't going to take me with him. I had to stay and look after Macedonia. Boring! I was already arguing with the old fool because he was trying to keep me in my place. He even had some of my friends banished from Macedonia.

Bucephalus carried me into all my battles. I even named a city after my faithful horse.

Murder in Macedonia

Then, at my sister's wedding of all places, Philip was murdered by one of his bodyguards. Obviously, we were all terribly upset, but it did make things a bit simpler. Philip's power games were a bit of a pain. With him out of the way, I could take on the top job.

Darius III

It wasn't just in Macedonia that being king was dangerous. Darius III (centre) came to lead the Persian Empire after the two previous kings had been killed. He may have ordered the murder of Philip to stop the Macedonian invasion of his lands.

Who murdered Philip?

The official story was that Philip's murderer, Pausanias, had a grudge against the king. But the people who had most to gain from his death were Alexander and his mother. Alexander and his father had argued and maybe Philip was planning to make someone else king after him. The historical mystery of whether Alexander killed his father will never be solved.

Master of Macedonia

The days after Philip's death were some of the most dangerous times in my whole life. There were plenty of powerful people who wanted to lead Macedonia. Some of them even thought I had arranged the murder of my father.

Once I was king, I couldn't wait to get out of Pella, Macedonia, and see the world.

The Macedonian army accepted me as king, which was a very good start. However, most people thought Philip's son (that's me) would be a bit of a pushover. There were rumblings of discontent everywhere.

Persian plans

I hadn't been brought up to spend my entire life ruling Macedonia. I needed to sort out my enemies close to home, and then I was planning to finish the job my father had started. I went to meet the Greek states and convinced them that I was the man to take revenge on the Persians for their past attacks on Greece.

You know you're really a king when they put your picture on the coins.

Document it!

How do you think Alexander felt when he became king of Macedonia? He could have written his feelings in a diary. Your private feelings about something may not be the same as what you tell people in public. Alexander may have had worries about whether he was ready to take over as king, but he would not have shown that to his soldiers.

"For being more bent upon action and glory than either upon pleasure or riches, he … would have chosen rather to succeed to a kingdom involved in troubles and wars, which would have afforded him frequent exercise of his courage…"

The Roman writer Plutarch explains Alexander's hunger for glory.

First fights

Before I could think about the Persians, I needed to make sure Macedonia was safe. I dealt with the revolting barbarians to the north and west of the country. These quick campaigns also proved to my Macedonian troops that I meant business.

The Greeks were supposed to be cultured and smart, and not at all like the barbarians of the north. But I soon discovered that some of them weren't so bright. The people of Thebes heard a rumour that I was dead. They soon realized their mistake when I returned to crush their silly little rebellion.

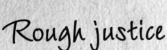

Rough justice

The Greek rebellions had to be stamped out once and for all. I ordered that all of Thebes had to be destroyed. The Greeks may not have liked me, but I never had as much trouble from them after that.

I had Thebes burnt to the ground.

The Macedonian army

There were probably more than 35,000 men in the Macedonian army when Alexander became king. They were the strongest and best-trained army in Europe. Greek armies normally used heavily armed foot soldiers called hoplites, but the Macedonians used fast-moving cavalry (soldiers on horseback) to break up enemy troop formations.

After the cavalry had broken the enemy lines, the heavily armed foot soldiers would go to work.

Greek grumbles

I really wanted the Greeks to like me. They always thought we Macedonians were beneath them, but I had been brought up as a Greek. It might take them a while to forgive me for destroying Thebes. Maybe if I could defeat the old enemy, Persia, they would realize that I was really on their side.

The Persians were also one enemy that my father never defeated. If I could defeat them, then I would be the one that everyone remembered. Philip who?

Leaving home

In spring 334 BC, I said goodbye to my homeland and my family. I did not know if I would ever return, and I did wonder what would happen if I didn't defeat the Persians. But I soon put these thoughts out of my mind as I led my forces towards the Persian Empire. My father's general Parmenion was already waiting for me at the Hellespont, the narrow strip of water where Europe meets Asia.

The Persian Empire

The Persian Empire stretched from the borders of India to Asia Minor (in modern Turkey). Under King Darius I, the Persians had attacked Athens and had been defeated at the Battle of Marathon. Although its power had declined by Alexander's time, the empire remained a powerful enemy.

I was never one to hang back
when it came to the battle. Here
I am attacking the Persians.

First steps into Asia

As I crossed the Hellespont and landed in Asia, I threw my spear into the ground. I wanted everyone to know I was here to stay. Of course, the Persians thought they could do something about that, and I faced them in the first battle at the Granicus River soon after we arrived. We won, of course, but King Darius was still building his army for the battle that could decide his fate, and mine.

Knot a problem

There was an old legend that whoever could untie an ancient knot at Gordium would rule Asia. I don't like to disappoint my people, so I said I'd have a go. It was really difficult, but I couldn't afford to fail. In the end, I drew my sword and sliced through it. I don't know why no one had thought of it before!

Dodgy Darius

We seemed to be making good progress, and I couldn't work out why Darius wasn't coming to fight. Finally, he managed to get his strongest forces together for a battle at Issus in autumn 333 BC. It was another big win for the Macedonians (with some added Greeks). Darius saved his own skin but left his family behind to fight. What a coward!

The great general

Alexander was one of the most successful generals in history. Some people say that he was lucky, but Alexander always made sure his battle plans suited the terrain, and targeted the weaknesses of his enemy. His soldiers followed him because he was always ready to put his own life in danger in the heat of the battle.

Dissing Darius

Darius offered me half of his empire to make peace with him. I told him I was having all of it, and I'd catch up with him too. I certainly had to fight for it.

One of my toughest battles was the siege of Tyre on the coast of Phoenicia (modern Lebanon). After many months, we stormed the island city by attacking from land and sea.

Egyptian holiday

At least the Egyptians were pleased to see me when I arrived at the end of 332 BC. They made me king of Egypt, and I made sure to respect their gods. I founded a city so the Greeks could trade with Egypt. Alexandria seemed like a fitting name.

Traditional boats on the River Nile have not changed much since I travelled to Egypt.

The best bit of my stay in Egypt was going across the desert to the Siwah Oasis. This was a very sacred place and I spoke to the oracle of the god Amon. It was good news. The oracle said I was the son of Amon, Egypt's top god, or the Greek version of Zeus. I'm not sure if I believed it myself, but it certainly helped to keep people on my side.

Ancient Egypt

When Alexander arrived in Egypt, the Egyptian civilization along the River Nile was already 3,000 years old. Ancient Egypt had been invaded by Persia in around 520 BC. The Persians had not been popular rulers, and Alexander was welcomed.

Hephaestion

Hephaestion was Alexander's closest friend throughout his life. He accompanied the king to Egypt and Asia, becoming commander of the cavalry. Alexander was deeply upset when his friend died in 324 BC.

Pursuing the Persians

I had a great time in Egypt, but after a few weeks of people being nice to me, I couldn't wait to get back on the battlefield. If we were going to finish off Darius, we would have to go deep into Asia, where no Greek or Macedonian army had ever been before.

Showdown

Well, we went looking for a fight, and we found one. The Persian army waited for us deep inside their territory. We finally met at the Battle of Gaugamela. The Persian army was much larger than ours, but we won a great victory. Darius, the so-called Great Persian King, once again ran for his life. Wimp!

It took me a while to capture King Darius because he kept running away.

With Darius hiding somewhere, I now ruled Persia. I then did something that none of my supporters expected. I put a Persian in charge of the city of Babylon. The Macedonians and Greeks thought I was going soft.

Parmenion

Parmenion had been Philip II's general. He took on the same job for Alexander, but was much more cautious than the fiery young king. Parmenion was old enough to be Alexander's grandfather. Once the defeat of Darius was complete, Alexander no longer needed him. In 330 BC, Alexander accused Parmenion's son of trying to kill him and had both father and son killed.

Occasionally, my men argued against me, but I stayed in control — for now.

"I will not demean myself by stealing victory like a thief."
Alexander's reply when Parmenion advised him to attack Darius's forces at night.

All work and no play

Winning battles was the easy part, apart from the danger of getting killed. After the defeat of Darius, I had to find ways to govern a huge empire, and that meant getting the Persians on my side. Otherwise, I'd have to deal with rebellions all the time.

It was a great feeling when we reached the Persian capital of Persepolis. Then I knew we'd really beaten them. It was the end of a long road, and I'm afraid we didn't behave very well. I now regret burning down the royal palace, but it showed who was boss. It was also revenge for Persian attacks on Greece in the past.

Persepolis was a great city, but Greek and Macedonian soldiers were not in a friendly mood after years of fighting against the Persians.

Still, there was no time to rest. I needed to make sure that Darius III was finally out of the way. He had fled to the far corner of the empire, so we followed. When we got to his hiding place in Bactria, we found that some guy called Bessus had already murdered the king and was claiming the crown for himself.

Document it!

Those who wrote about him during his life had a favourable view of Alexander. If not, they might have found themselves in trouble. When looking at writing from the past, you should always think about whether the writer is giving a fair view or just giving one side of the argument. Think about this in your own writing, too.

"Through the gift of the gods I am now in possession of the country ... and now that I am lord and master of all Asia, come to me..."

Alexander's letter to Darius III, 333 BC.

Finding new lands

The Persian Empire did not end in Persepolis. It had once stretched as far as the Indus River. When I told the army that we were heading further east, they weren't happy. Every step we made was into new and unexplored land. It had been many years since the soldiers had seen their homes and families, and they were homesick.

Losing the plot

There were even plots to get rid of me, their glorious leader. I used one as an excuse to kill my father's old general Parmenion and his son. The army needed new blood in charge, so a bit of old blood had to be spilled.

The high mountains of the Hindu Kush tested my army's strength and toughness.

The first job was to teach the upstart Bessus a lesson. We followed him across the high mountains of the Hindu Kush. Finally, we caught up with Bessus. It was probably a bit harsh to cut off his nose and ears before killing him, but that was the Persian custom.

Beyond the Persian Empire

The Persian Empire had once stretched as far as India, but the Persians had been pushed back by local leaders before Alexander arrived. Alexander faced fierce warriors whom he knew little about. These lands were all new to the Macedonians, and they also found natural hazards such as mountains, fast-flowing rivers, and barren deserts.

Document it!

Alexander was exploring new things all the time. New experiences are great topics to write about in a journal, even if it's something really normal like visiting a new city or discovering a new favourite band or film.

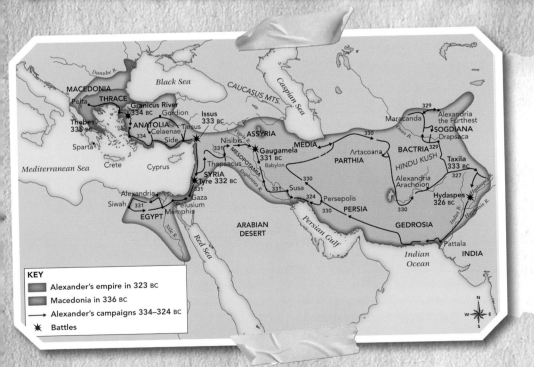

My campaigns in Asia took me to lands where no European army had ever been before.

KEY
- Alexander's empire in 323 BC
- Macedonia in 336 BC
- → Alexander's campaigns 334–324 BC
- ★ Battles

...ets

...sible that all the success went to my head a bit.
...f my army certainly thought so. One of my commanders, Cleitus, claimed that I should be more humble and give some credit to my father for my success. I was angry, but maybe I shouldn't have killed him. I guess having the power to do absolutely anything you want is not necessarily a good thing. Remember, although I'd conquered half the world, I wasn't even 30 years old yet.

One thing I learned in India was to keep clear of the rampaging war elephants.

Into India

But there was no time for moping around. India was waiting. There, we faced the war elephants of the great warrior Porus at the Battle of the Hydaspes River. Although we won the battle, I was impressed by Porus and left him in charge of his lands.

My plan was to keep going into the new lands, but my army let me down. They just refused to go any further. I was furious, but there wasn't much I could do. We built a fleet of ships on the Hydaspes River that carried us to the coast along other Indian rivers. From there, we endured a terrible march back across the desert to Persia. No army could defeat me, but the hot, dry desert nearly finished off my troops.

This silver medal was made to mark my victories in India.

Nearchus

Nearchus had travelled with Alexander from Greece. He was put in charge of a fleet of 150 ships that explored the coast of the Indian Ocean and carried part of the army to meet up with Alexander after his desert march.

The end of the march

In 325 BC, my campaigns were over, at least for now. The army was tired and many of the soldiers were getting old. I also needed to start ruling rather than just adding new lands to my empire. The problem with conquering people is you make an awful lot of enemies. I always had to watch my back. I didn't know whom to trust. Peace was a lot more difficult than war.

People often ask me what makes a great general. I believe it's important to listen to those around you but, once a decision is taken, I always act ruthlessly. I had to kill some of my most trusted generals when they questioned my authority.

Moaning Macedonians

I tried to get the Macedonians and Persians to mingle. Many of my closest companions married Persians, but most of the Macedonians were not convinced. In the end, I told my army to go home if they didn't like it. I was staying in Asia.

> *"Some of the [soldiers] brought a litter to carry the king ... but he refused it and ordered that his horse be brought alongside. When next he was seen, he was mounted on the horse, and at this the whole army applauded wildly, over and over again."*

Alexander was injured fighting in India, but did not want to show any weakness to his army.

I was a powerful leader and
conquered many lands.

Back to Babylon

When I reached the city of Babylon, with its beautiful gardens, I didn't really believe my conquering days were over. After all, I was only 32 years old, still much too young to retire. Many of the greatest generals hadn't even started by my age. With a new, younger army I could go back to explore India again.

By 323 BC, I had conquered a great empire and was ready to start ruling it. There would always be more places to explore and conquer, but there did not seem much point if it all fell apart when you died. I needed someone who could take over the empire from me. I had certainly come a long way from Macedonia, but there was still a lot to do.

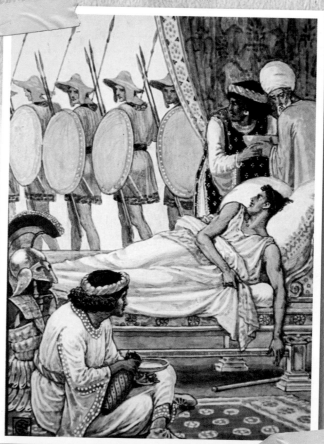

Alexander on his deathbed. The great king certainly made lots of enemies who might have wanted to murder him.

Was Alexander murdered?

Alexander died in Babylon on 11 June 323 BC. No one can be sure why. Alexander was incredibly fit and strong, but he could have caught an illness. Some experts think that Alexander was murdered like his father, possibly with poison. The murderer could have been one of his companions who bore a grudge or who feared that he might be dismissed or executed by the king.

Roxane

Roxane married Alexander to seal an alliance between him and her family, who ruled lands in central Asia. Roxane was the mother of Alexander's son, who was born after the death of his father. Roxane and young Alexander were both killed in the wars that followed the death of Alexander the Great.

This picture was painted long after Alexander died. In fact, he never met his son, who was also called Alexander.

Alexander's place in history

Many people saw Alexander as a god while he was still alive. More than 2,300 years after he died, it still seems incredible that, in a few short years, the young king could have conquered such a huge empire. But Alexander did not live long enough to test whether the empire could last, and so his work was left unfinished.

We can only guess whether Alexander would have been able to hold his empire together. He certainly had a big impact on all those who followed him, as he built bridges between the civilizations of Europe and Asia. His military campaigns spread Greek culture across a huge area, and he founded more than 70 cities across the empire.

But Alexander's main impact was probably his amazing strength and fighting spirit. He inspired many later generals, from Julius Caesar to Napoleon, to believe that they could match his success.

> *"I cannot determine with certainty what sort of plans Alexander had in mind, but none was small and petty, and he would not have stopped conquering even if he'd added Europe to Asia and the British Isles to Europe."*
>
> Arrian, a Roman who wrote Alexander's biography 500 years after his death (AD 177).

Roman generals like Julius Caesar were inspired by Alexander as they built their own great empire. They also created many statues of Alexander.

What happened to Alexander's empire?

Alexander's empire was made up of Macedonians, Greeks, Egyptians, and many different peoples within the Persian Empire. They were only held together by Alexander's rule. After his death, the generals appointed Alexander's infant son and his half brother Philip Arrhidaeus as joint kings. However, in a few years, both had been murdered, and Alexander's empire had separated into several different states.

Timeline

356 BC   Alexander is born around 20 July

344   Alexander tames the horse Bucephalus

343   Aristotle is Alexander's tutor

340   Alexander becomes Regent of Macedonia while Philip II is away fighting

336   Philip II is assassinated at his daughter's wedding. Alexander comes to power in Macedonia.

335   Campaigns against Macedonia's enemies, including destruction of Thebes

334   Alexander crosses the Hellespont to begin his conquest of Persia

  (May) Battle of the River Granicus

333   (November) Battle of Issus; Persian King Darius III's family captured by Alexander

332   Siege of Tyre, Phoenicia

  Alexander founds Alexandria in Egypt, and visits oracle at Siwah Oasis

331   (1 October) Battle of Gaugamela and final defeat of Darius III's forces

330   Alexander burns royal palace at Persepolis

  Execution of Philotas and murder of his father Parmenion

Write your own journal

Alexander probably didn't have much time for writing a journal. He was always on the march to the next battle. It was left to other people to write about his amazing achievements and to guess about what motivated the great conqueror.

You may not be planning to build an empire covering half the world, but keeping a journal about your own life can still be great fun. A public journal or blog lets you explain your views and ideas to other people. Here are some tips on keeping a journal.

- **Who's going to read it?** Before you start, is the journal just for yourself or do you want others to read it? The words you use and the things you write may be very different, depending on what you choose.

- **Where will you write your journal?** You may want to write by hand in a notebook, or type your journal on a computer. If you want to share your journal, there are many websites where you can set up a blog. If you choose this, be careful to stay safe online and never give out personal information about yourself and other people to strangers. This includes your real name, age, address, and the school you go to.

- **What else can you include?** You may be happy just to include your words in the journal, but there are lots of other media you can include, such as photos, letters, and emails, or links to websites if you're working online. You may even want to include video or audio recordings. If you're writing a blog or public journal, always ask for permission first before including emails from other people, or photos showing them.

- **You could also record a video journal.** Even if you do this, you still need to think about things like your audience and the words you use to express yourself. Make some notes beforehand so you know what you're going to cover and your video diary is easy to follow.

- **Make sure you keep writing your journal.** Lots of people start a diary at the beginning of the year and stop after a few days or weeks. Set aside a time each day for writing your journal. Ask yourself a question every time you write to help you get ideas for journal entries; for example:

  - What were the best and worst things that happened today?

  - What was happening in the world today, such as news stories that had an impact on you?

  - If you were reading this journal in 100 years' time, what would you want to know about?

Glossary

ambition goal or success that someone wants to achieve

authority the power or right to make decisions and give orders to other people

barbarians people who lived outside ancient Greece and did not share Greek culture

barren describes land that is too poor to produce plants or crops

bodyguard guard who protects an important person

cavalry soldiers fighting on horseback

city-state in ancient Greece, a city and the land that surrounded it

companion friend. The word was used to describe Alexander's closest friends and also parts of the Macedonian army.

conquer invade or take over a country by force

cultured knowing about and appreciating things such as art and music

cunning misleading or deceiving someone to get what you want

empire lands controlled or governed from a foreign country

found build or establish something, such as a city or organization

legend traditional story that may be true in parts but can't be proved

murder kill someone deliberately

oracle place or shrine where ancient people believed they could ask questions and receive answers from their gods

Persian Empire empire founded in what is now Iran by Cyrus the Great, which came to control large parts of Asia before being defeated by Alexander

rebellion uprising of people against their leaders or government

regent someone appointed to rule if the actual ruler is too young or not able to rule

retire stop working or leave one's job, usually because of age

rival opponent or enemy

ruthless willing to use extreme means to get what you want

sacred connected with a god; holy

siege when enemy forces surround a town or other community, cutting off supplies in order to get the people inside to surrender

terrain landscape

troop soldiers; cavalry unit

Find out more

Books

Alexander the Great (Lives in Action), Martin Howard
(A & C Black, 2010)

Alexander the Great: the Life of a King and a Conqueror,
Anita Ganeri and Rob Shone (Book House, 2005)

Avoid Being in Alexander the Great's Army (The Danger Zone),
Jacqueline Morley and David Antram (Book House, 2006)

In the Footsteps of Alexander the Great, Michael Wood
(BBC Books, 2004)
This book is aimed at adults but accompanies a fascinating TV
series (available on DVD) that retraces the steps of Alexander's
campaigns.

Websites

www.bbc.co.uk/news/magazine-18803290
Not everyone thought Alexander was great! This article
gives the Persian point of view.

www.livius.org/aj-al/alexander/alexander00.html
This website has a detailed biography of Alexander and
his campaigns.

Places to visit

There are many historical sites linked to Alexander in Eastern
Europe, Asia, and Egypt, but sites such as the ruins of
Persepolis in Iran are not accessible to most people. Other
sites, such as Alexandria in Egypt, have been built over so
there is little trace of Alexander.

The World Heritage Site at Aigai in northern Greece is the site
of Macedonia's ancient capital. Sites such as the Acropolis of
Athens and museum exhibits around the world will give you a
great understanding of the world that produced Alexander.

Topics for further research

- Ancient Greek warfare: Alexander's defeat of Persia was just the latest battle between the Greek world and the Persians. Find out more about other battles between them, such as the battles of Marathon and Salamis.

- Find out more about the civilizations of central Asia, such as the Persian Empire and the people of the Indus Valley.

- How do you think Alexander changed the world? Make a list of ways that he influenced history. What do you think he might have done if he hadn't died at such a young age?

Index